JAZZ UP YOUR CHRISTMAS

At The Piano

Twelve Christmas Carols in a Fresh Perspective

Arranged by Lee Evans

T0053169

CONTENTS

Foreword

This volume of famous Christmas carols offers a fresh perspective in the jazz idiom to these familiar holiday materials.

The extensive fingering provided herein is intended to enable the pianist to best capture characteristic keyboard jazz phrasing, and it is strongly urged that fingerings, pedal indications, and interpretive markings (staccatos, accents, etc.) be strictly observed.

The entire book, or portions of it, may be played as a concert suite.

L.E.

Second Edition

THE COMPOSER GRATEFULLY ACKNOWLEDGES THE INVALUABLE EDITORIAL ASSISTANCE PROVIDED BY MARCIA KLEBANOW FOR THIS BOOK.

EDWARD B. Marks Music Company / Exclusively Distributed By HAL•LEONARD CORPORATION

DECK THE HALLS

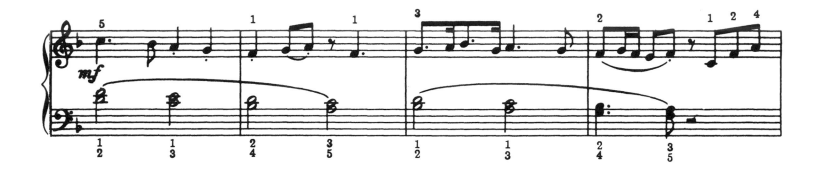

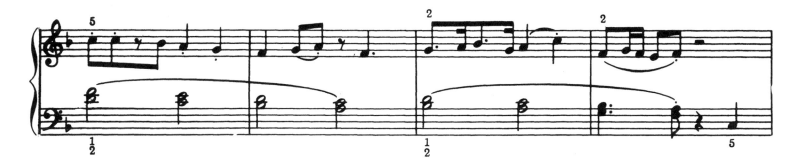

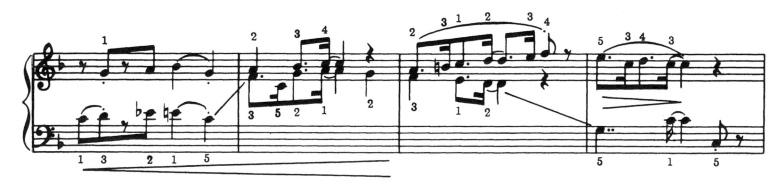

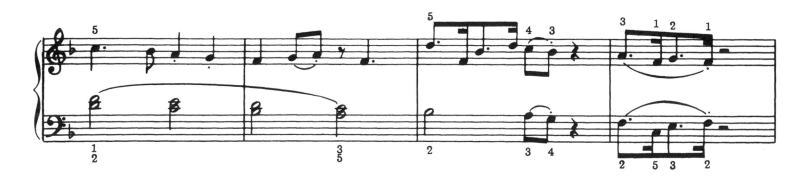

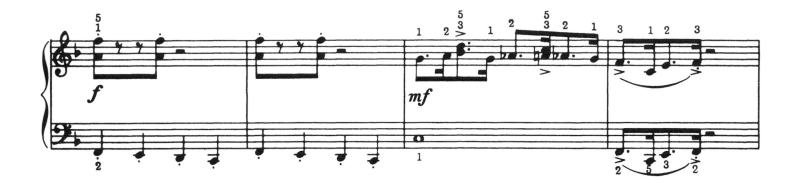

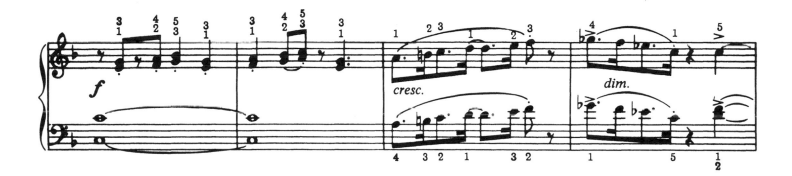

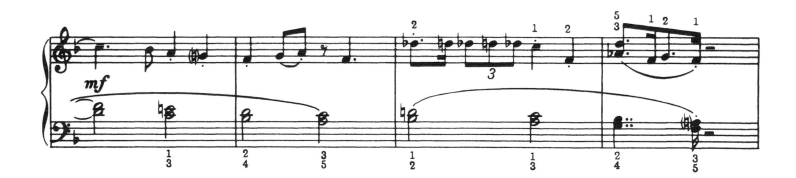

WE WISH YOU A MERRY CHRISTMAS

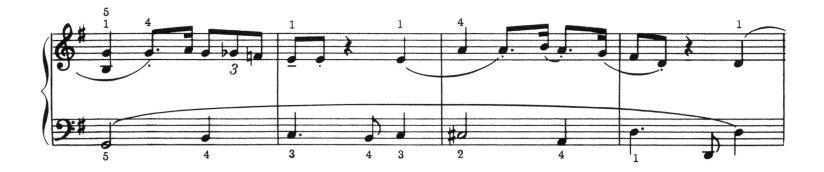

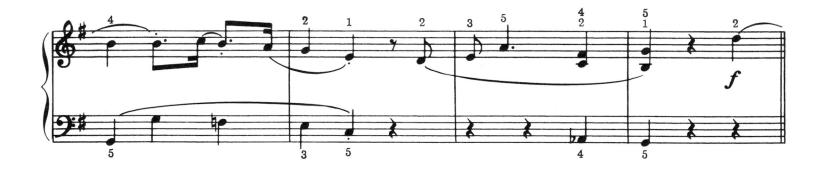

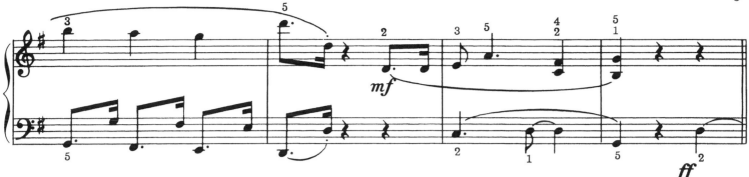

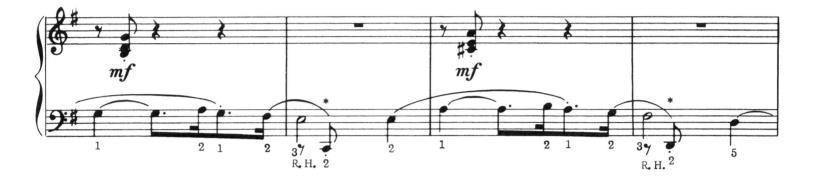

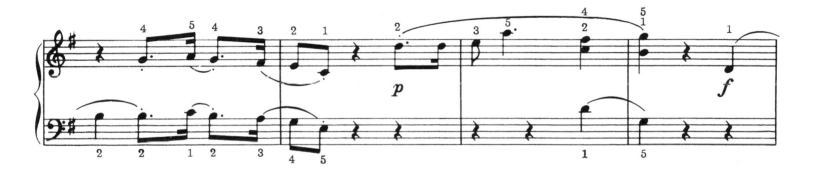

* Cross hands

Ped.———

JINGLE BELLS

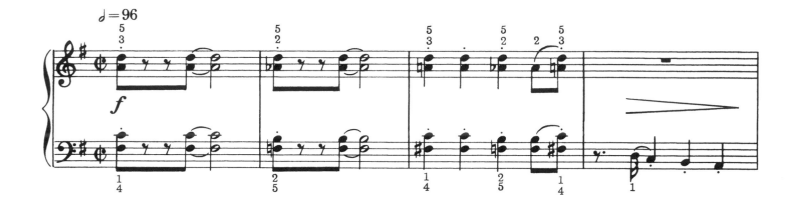

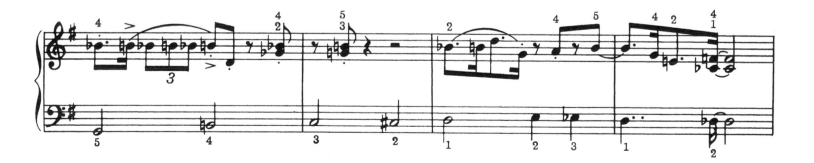

HERE WE COME A-WASSAILING

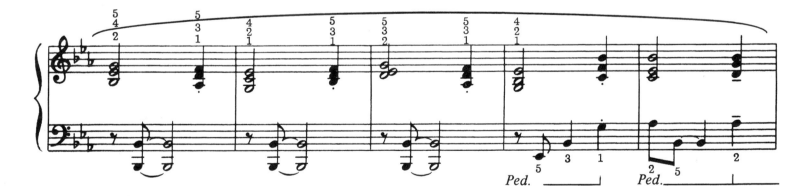

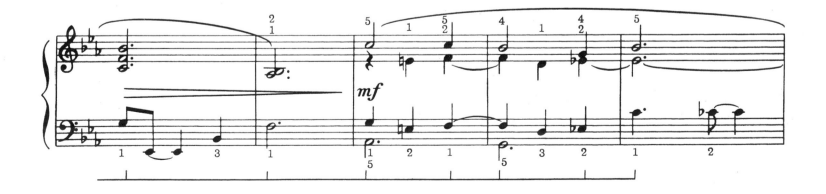

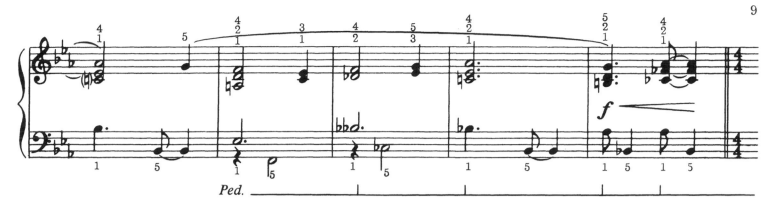

L'istesso tempo*

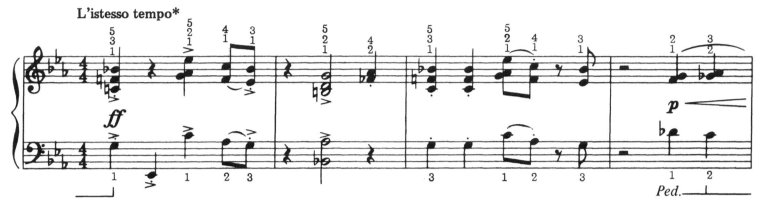

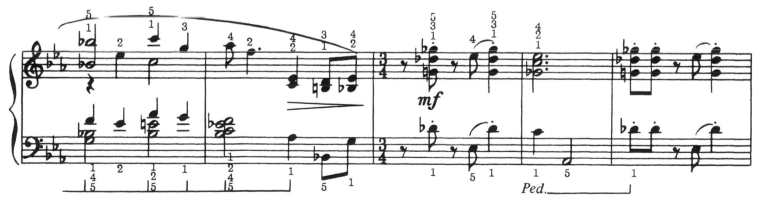

* L'istesso tempo = same tempo

SILENT NIGHT

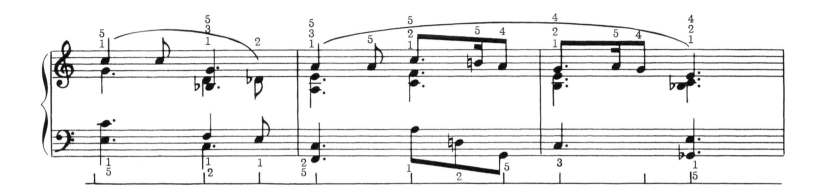

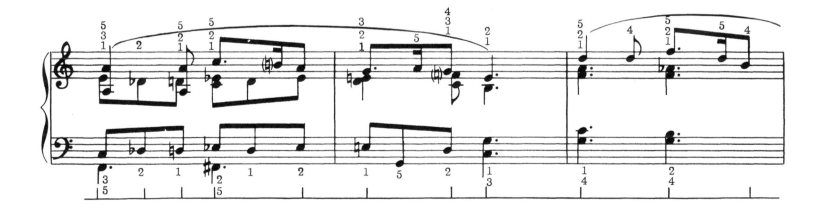

O CHRISTMAS TREE

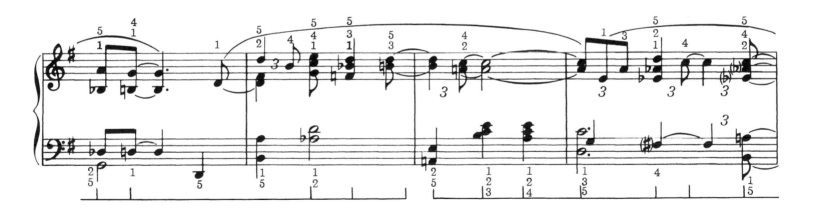

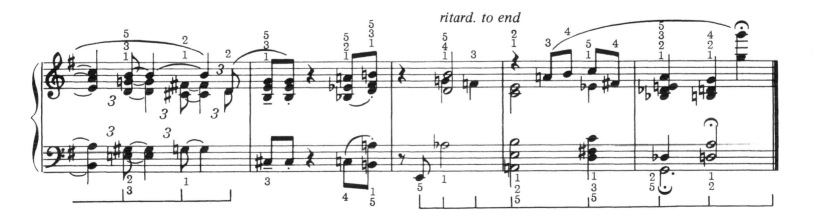

15974-22

WHAT CHILD IS THIS? (GREENSLEEVES)

♩ = 108

Delicately and expressively

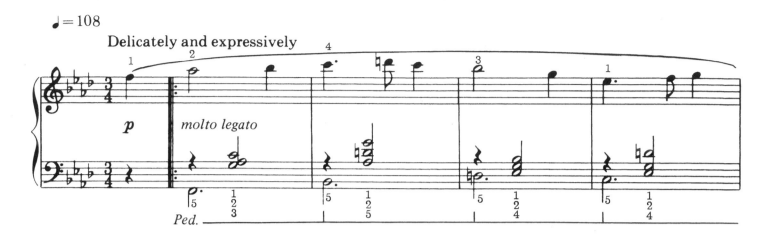

p   *molto legato*

Ped.

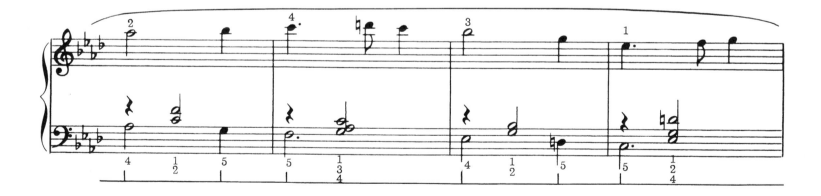

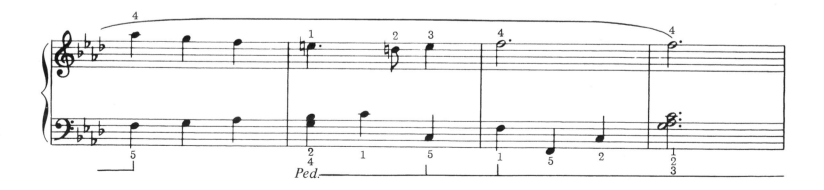

Ped.

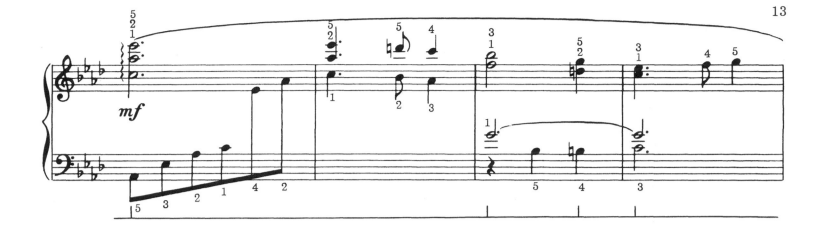

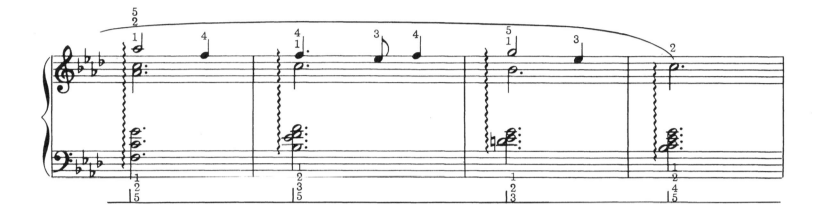

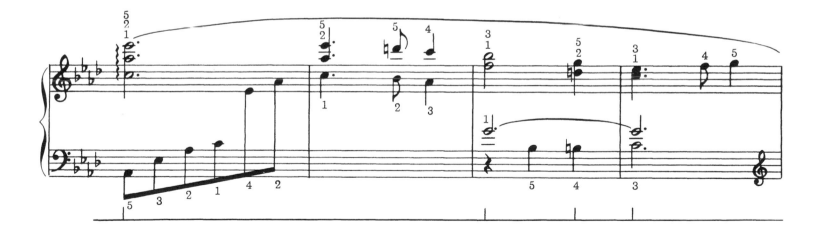

THE FIRST NOEL

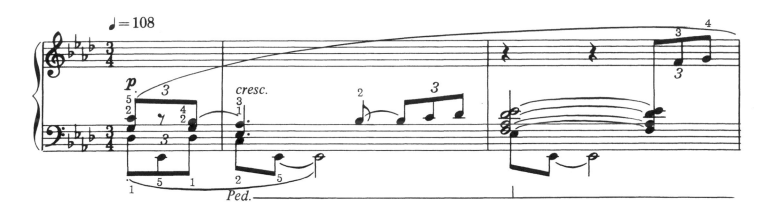

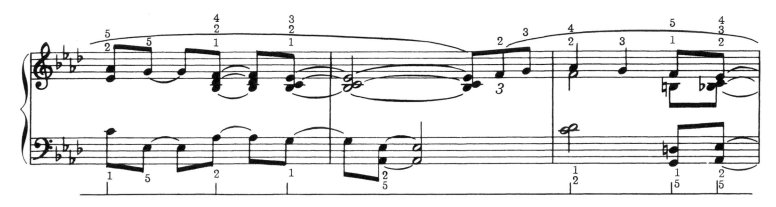

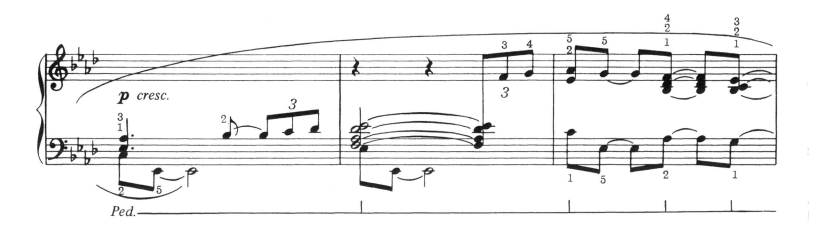

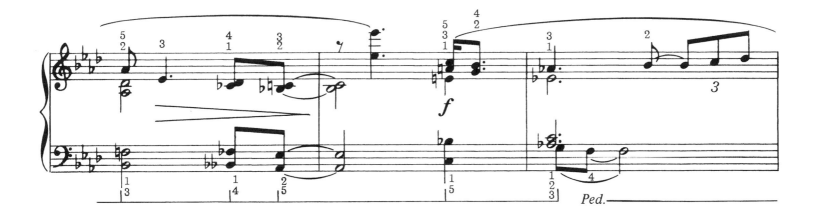

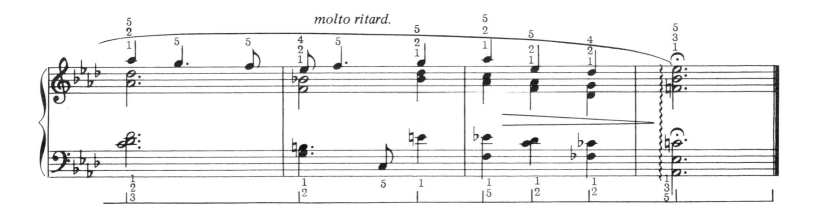

IT CAME UPON A MIDNIGHT CLEAR

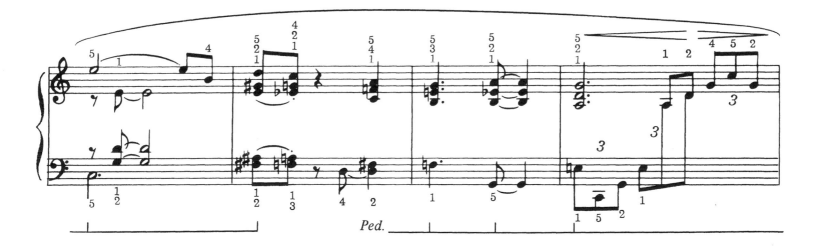

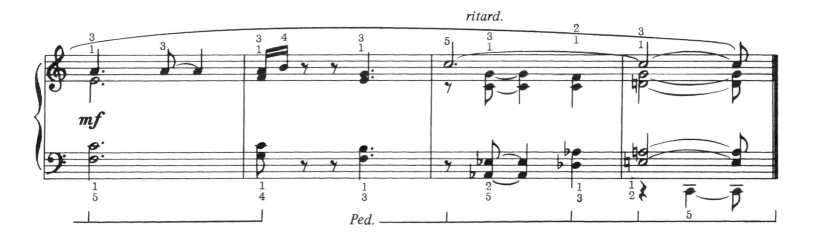

THE HOLLY AND THE IVY

(English)

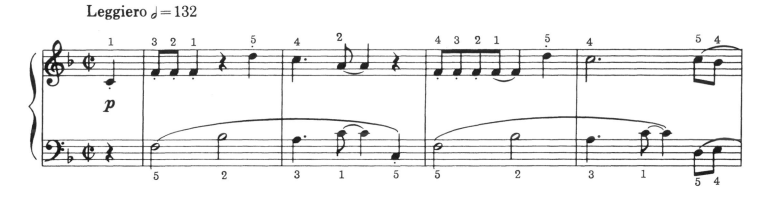

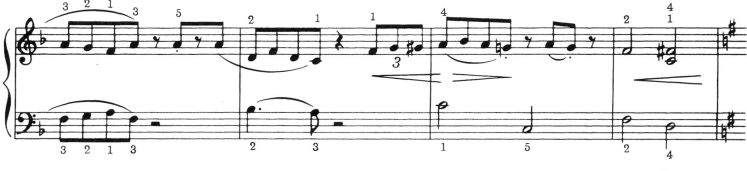

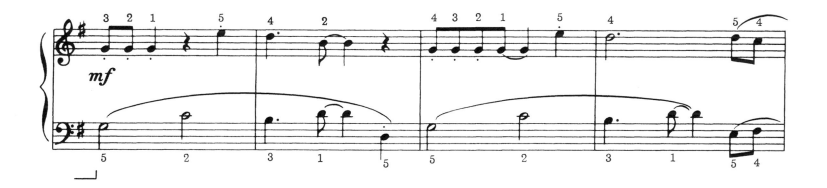

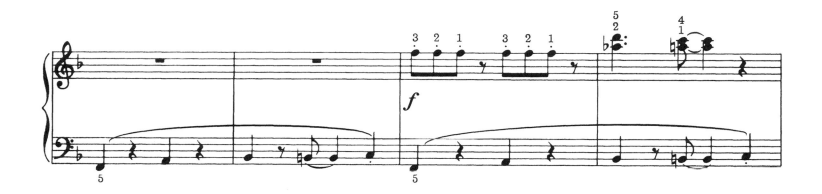

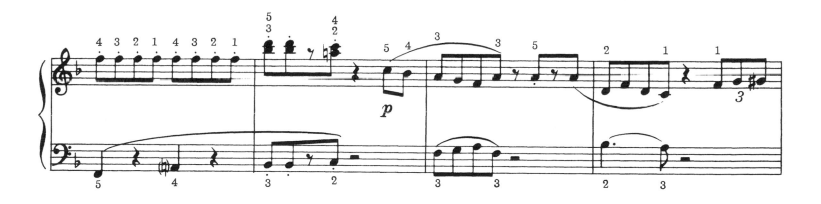

GOD REST YE MERRY, GENTLEMEN

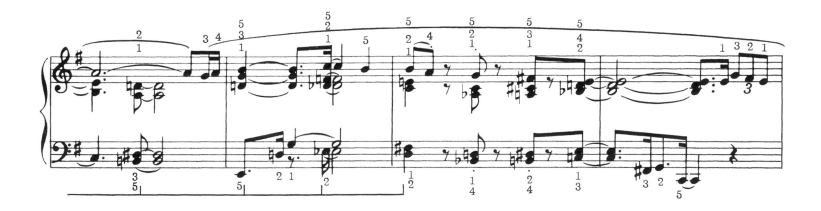

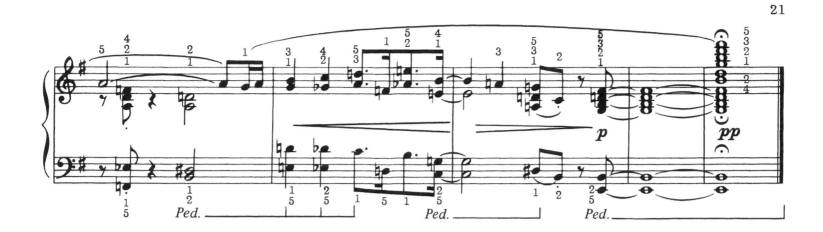

DING DONG, MERRILY ON HIGH

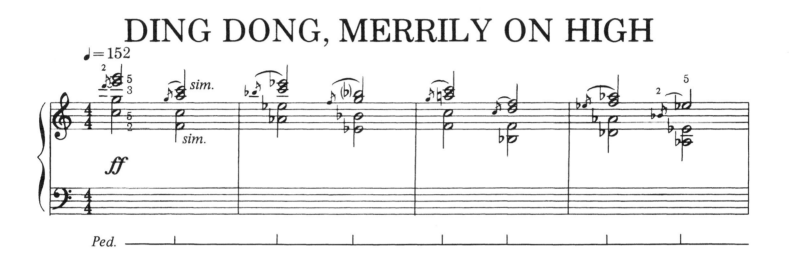

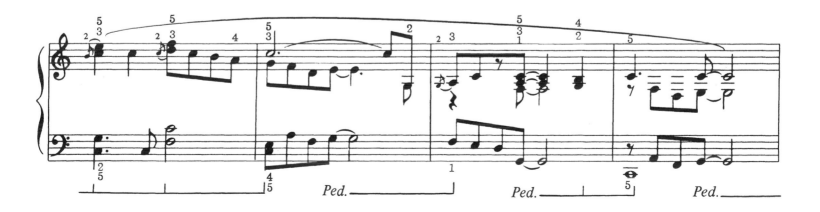

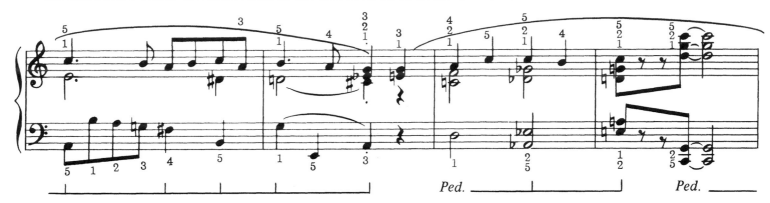

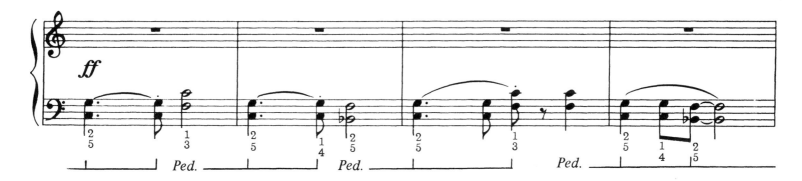

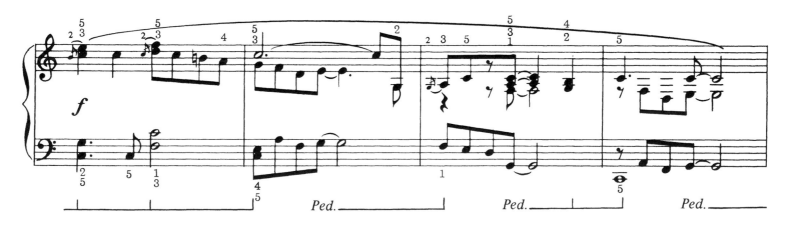

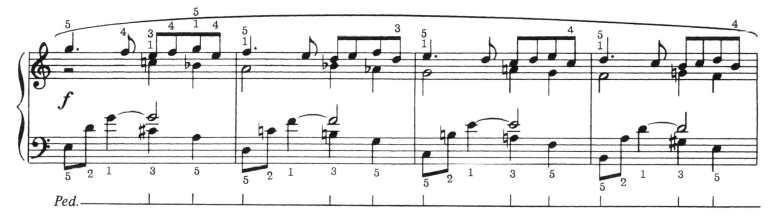

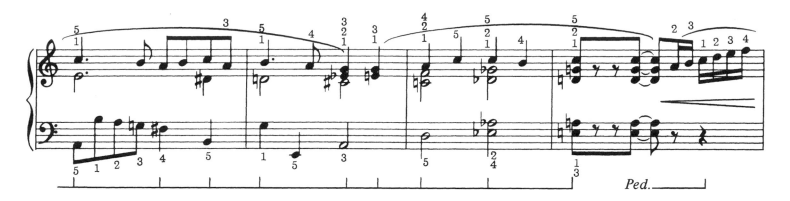

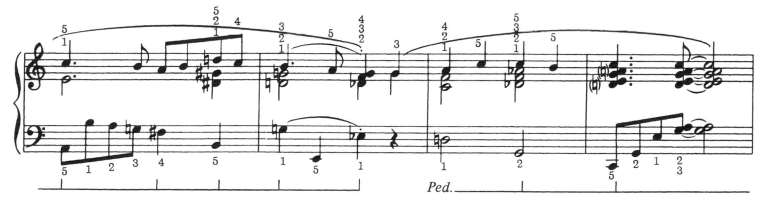